Retire with knowledge

How to gain financial strength
so you can serve God's kingdom

Viazadora (VeVe) Saunders

Contents

Author Bio

VeVe is a passionate minister on a mission to express her profound love and devotion to God, with an unwavering dedication to enrich, empower, and positively impact the lives of others. With a wealth of experience in the financial industry, having worked with some of the world's top financial firms, VeVe's spiritual journey led her to a deeper calling. Seeking a greater understanding and a desire to contribute more to the kingdom of God, VeVe pursued her studies at Charis Bible College, graduating in 2021. Following her graduation, VeVe's creative spirit flourished as she wrote 7 soul-stirring songs, channeling her faith and experiences into uplifting melodies. Furthermore, she embarked on a remarkable venture by founding Kingdom Health and Wealth, a visionary platform committed to providing invaluable educational resources and tailored Christian coaching to enrich every aspect of life. VeVe's relentless pursuit to spread the Good News about God's love and grace serves as the cornerstone of her inspiring journey.

Dedication

VeVe has over 20 years of experience in the financial industry she would like to dedicate this information to all those who are in need of guidance in retirement planning, drawing from her personal and professional experience with the hope of helping others prepare for retirement.

Following the second greatest commandment, given by God to love thy neighbor as thy self. Matthews 22:39.

Retire with knowledge

*How to gain financial strength
so you can serve Gods kingdom*

When most of us think about retirement, we envision it as the most promising time of our lives—a time to relax and enjoy life with the financial means to do so. Unfortunately, many Americans are not on track for a secure retirement or are simply unprepared. This book aims to provide insight to help you gain a fundamental understanding of retirement planning. It's important not to get discouraged upon learning the real facts about today's retirement statistics. Instead, this information is meant to encourage you to make concrete plans for your retirement life and understand the truth about it. It is God's purpose for you to be with knowledge, and for you to be blessed.

> Jeremiah 29: 11
> "for I know the thoughts that I think towards
> you said the Lord thoughts of peace, and not
> of evil to give you an expected end"

Introduction

Before diving into the details, I'd like to share my personal story and how I've witnessed firsthand the hardships that can arise from not planning for retirement.

A Look Back at Family and Retirement

Growing up in New York as part of an average working family, I witnessed the dedication of both my parents as they toiled throughout my childhood and young adult life. I distinctly recall the pivotal moment when my father, having dedicated over 25 years of service to the New York Transit Authority, announced his decision to retire. Similarly, my mother, who had devoted two decades to the New York Telephone Company, also opted for retirement around the same time.

During those years, it was common for companies to offer Pension Plans. For those unfamiliar with this term, an employer pension plan is a specific type of retirement plan in which the employer makes contributions on behalf of the employees, ensuring a guaranteed income during the employees' retirement years. The plan did not require the employee to contribute any money.

Unfortunately, employer-only contribution pension plans are nearly nonexistent in today's world. When my father, at 55 years of age, made the decision to retire, he held the belief that his pension plan, coupled with personal savings, would afford him a comfortable retirement. With this in mind, my parents made the choice to relocate from New York to North Carolina, seeking what many would consider a good retirement. They purchased a house and started traveling they were truly enjoying their retirement years. Then, the unforeseen occurred: my mother suffered a brain aneurysm, necessitating extensive medical care. This medical crisis swiftly depleted all of my parents' savings and plunged them into financial hardship. In just four years, the situation escalated to the point where my parents lost their home and were compelled to relocate to an apartment. Watching my mother go through a long and expensive recovery, I saw their planned retirement change from a happy dream to a financial disaster. Unfortunately my mother did not have medical insurance.

This information aims to equip you with the knowledge necessary to prepare for your retirement years, outlining strategies to plan for unforeseen situations and offering guidance on achieving a comfortable retirement.

Initiating a retirement plan requires careful consideration and prayer of three fundamental questions: When do I want to retire? What lifestyle do I envision for my retirement years? And how will I achieve this goal financially? By addressing these important factors and prayerfully seeking God for guidance you will embark on the initial steps of your retirement planning journey.

When you're thinking about when to retire, it's important to be practical. Two main things to think about are: first, deciding the best age for you to retire, and second, figuring out where you want to live during your retirement. Even if you're not sure about these things right now, it's good to start thinking about what age you might want to retire and where you'd like to live. As time goes on, you'll get a clearer idea, and having a good plan will be really helpful.

When preparing for your retirement, it is essential to capitalize on your employer's retirement savings plan, if available. Traditional pension plans have it's almost unheard of however many employers provide options such as 401(k), 403(b), 457, SIMPLE, and SEP retirement plans. These plans typically require contributions from you, with the potential for additional contributions from your employer. It is very important not to overlook this opportunity for additional funds, so aim to contribute at least enough to receive the full employer match—Do your best not to give away free money.

For those who are self-employed or lack access to an employer-sponsored retirement savings plan, there are numerous avenues for establishing individual retirement plans. These include options such as a Roth IRA, a traditional IRA, annuities, and even a SEP IRA, This allows you to put more money in for a certain amount of time, so you can save more.

Whether you have an employer-sponsored plan or are self-employed, personal savings play a vital role in retirement planning. This information is meant to provide simple ways to save money to help you reach your goals.

When determining the age at which you want to retire it is crucial to select an age that aligns with your comfort and financial preparedness. To provide a realistic example, working for an employer the average retirement age falls within the range of 60 to 65, with a significant portion of Americans retiring around 62. However, if you opt for retirement before the age of 65, it is very important to thoroughly consider your medical insurance benefits. Medical expenses represent a substantial cost for many individuals during their retirement years.

Upon reaching the age of 65, most Americans become eligible for Medicare, a federal healthcare insurance program. It's important to know that some of the money taken from your paycheck goes to Medicare and Social Security. So, it's a good idea to think about retiring at age 65, unless you have a strong medical plan in place for yourself if you retire before age 65. By maintaining a healthy lifestyle, including proper nutrition, regular exercise, and diligent healthcare, retiring at 65 can be a seamless and advantageous decision for your well-being.

Regrettably, many employers do not include continued medical coverage as part of their retirement plans.

Furthermore, the cost of living will significantly impact your financial situation during retirement. When determining your desired location for retirement, whether it be a specific city or state, opting for an area with a low to moderate cost of living can greatly benefit your financial circumstances. For instance, the cost of living in New York City is notably higher than that of Dallas, Texas.

Should you choose not to relocate during your retirement years, it is imperative to be well-prepared to afford the cost of living in your current city and state. Being mindful of both the age at which you plan to retire and the location in which you intend to reside holds substantial importance in your retirement planning.

Planning Your Retirement Lifestyle

It's important to think about the life you want during retirement. Your lifestyle choices will determine how much money you'll need. Some people dream of traveling, while others just want to live comfortably or make sure they can cover their bills. Whatever your dream is, the key to a good retirement is knowing what you want.

By understanding what you want for your retirement, you can make a plan that fits your goals.

Planning Your Finances for Retirement

After you've thought about the life you want in retirement, it's time to make a financial plan and set achievable goals for how you'll have enough money. Remember, these are the years when you won't be earning a regular paycheck.

Having a plan for how you'll set yourself up financially for retirement is key to successful and stress-free retirement living. In the next chapters, we'll help you understand how to set realistic goals and create a strong financial strategy that matches your retirement dreams.

Taking Steps Toward a Secure Retirement

Now, let's talk about how you can prepare yourself financially for retirement. Many people find the idea of saving for retirement overwhelming, especially with the rising cost of living, job insecurity, and everyday financial pressures.

To set yourself on the right track for a good retirement, consider these five steps. First, take a moment to figure out how much you can realistically save. For those with employer retirement plans, make the most of any matching programs they offer. For example, if your employer matches 3% of your contribution, make sure to contribute at least 3% from your paycheck, effectively doubling your savings to 6%. This means you won't miss out on the free money. Also, remember that contributing to your employer plan is usually done before taxes, so it won't have a big impact on your paycheck most people don't miss the money.

If you don't have access to an employer's retirement savings plan, consider starting a simple savings plan with an Individual Retirement Account (IRA). Many local banks and some credit unions allow you to start with as little as $50 per month, and there are investment companies with no minimum investment requirement.

The key to retirement planning is to start, regardless of whether you're 21 years old or 55 years old. If you think you can't afford to save, take a close look at your spending. If you can set aside at least $12 per week or $50 per month into a savings account, you can start planning for your retirement savings. This is just a basic start, and the more you can save, the more you can build wealth. If you haven't started yet, I recommend beginning your savings plan today.

Taking Control of Your Finances Through Budgeting

Once you've started saving for retirement, it's important to have a written budget to understand where your money is going and what you're spending it on. If you're unsure about where your money went after getting paid, it's likely because you don't have a written budget or didn't stick to it. The worst feeling is not knowing what happened to your hard-earned money. Take control of your finances by creating a budget. Having a clear budget, or at the very least knowing where your money is going, is a significant aspect of being financially prepared for retirement. It's crucial to be in control of your money.

Safeguarding Your Financial Future with Emergency Savings

As you prepare for retirement, it is crucial to consider unexpected circumstances that may arise. Each of us will encounter life's "What If" scenarios, making the establishment of an emergency savings fund imperative. An emergency savings fund provides protection from unforeseen events, both in the present and during retirement.

Unforeseen expenses are a common occurrence, and being prepared is essential. I recommend starting with a minimum of $1,000 for your emergency savings, but the general guideline is to have three to six months' worth of living expenses set aside. To calculate this, your monthly bills by three will give you the amount you should strive to save, providing a safety net for genuine emergency situations.

While saving may be challenging for many, starting with just $12 per week, which amounts to $50 per month, can set you on the path to building a strong emergency fund over time. This fund will serve as genuine protection in the event of a financial crisis. If you haven't yet started an emergency savings fund, I strongly encourage you to begin today.

Strive to be debt free

The next crucial step is to address your financial situation and prioritize becoming debt-free. Debt can significantly impact our financial well-being, particularly in the case of credit card debt, which affects a majority of Americans. Being in debt can hinder your ability to fully enjoy the fruits of our labor, ultimately impeding prosperity. It is imperative to recognize that debt poses a crisis in America, and many individuals unwittingly fall victim to its grasp.

Credit card offers may seem attractive because they allow you to buy now and pay later. However, this can lead to a long time of repaying the debt, and the amount you owe can grow rapidly. This creates a cycle where you are burdened with debt for a long time. Having this debt can be stressful.

For instance, consider that if you were to spend $1,000 on an average credit card and only make minimum payments, it would take approximately 62 months to fully settle the balance. This equates to just over five years to repay a $1,000 debt. Consequently, significant funds are diverted toward debt repayment, funds that could otherwise have been allocated towards savings, including retirement planning.

To embark on the journey to financial freedom, it is essential to set a clear goal of attaining a debt-free lifestyle. Begin by targeting the card with the highest interest rate and allocate additional funds towards reducing its balance, while maintaining minimum payments on other cards, assuming multiple debts are held. Once the first card is cleared, redirect the surplus funds toward the next outstanding balance or debt.

It is paramount to commit to every effort in order to establish a lifestyle free from the burden of debt. Remain vigilant against misleading offers and steadfastly pursue a debt-free future. Achieving financial freedom and prosperity is within reach when you are debt-free. The amount of money lost to credit card debt is staggering, and to prepare for a secure retirement, it is essential to eliminate this type of debt and avoid falling back into it. Start taking steps towards a debt-free life today.

How much will you need

The foundation of retirement planning involves estimating the amount of income you'll need and how long it will last. Research suggests that aiming for about 80% of your pre-retirement income can provide a comfortable retirement. For example, if you earn $60,000 per year before retirement, targeting around $48,000 per year during retirement may be sustainable.

When considering your retirement income needs, think about factors like ongoing mortgage or rent payments, potential medical expenses, and any outstanding debts. Understanding these factors will help you set a realistic savings goal. With good planning, you can work toward securing your financial future.

Making your money work for you

The final step in securing your financial future is to focus on investing for the long term. Once you have addressed any outstanding debt and have a clear understanding of your retirement income needs, it's time to consider how to grow your wealth and make your money work for you.

Investing for the future involves putting your money into assets that have the potential to increase in value over time, such as stocks, bonds, mutual funds, and real estate. By investing wisely, you can aim to build a nest egg that will support you throughout your retirement years.

Diversification is key to a successful investment strategy. By spreading your investments across different asset classes and sectors, you can help manage risk and maximize potential returns. It's also important to consider your risk tolerance and investment timeframe when making investment decisions.

If you need assistance with retirement planning, there are several options to consider. If you have an employer-sponsored retirement plan, I recommend taking advantage of any free seminars or human resource meetings your company offers on retirement planning.

For those who are self-employed or do not have access to an employer retirement plan, I suggest meeting with a representative at your local bank or credit union, as they often provide guidance to their clients.

Another option is to seek advice from a financial advisor. When choosing a financial advisor, it's important to look for a reputable company, although it's worth noting that there is usually a fee involved for their services. However, a financial advisor can help you understand and make smart choices about your money for the future. They know a lot about investing and can guide you in ways that will benefit your long-term financial health.

The reality is Retirement should be a rewarding phase of life, and it's up to you to make it happen. By taking these steps to plan for retirement, you can ensure that you're ready for this important stage in your life.

In conclusion It's not just about money during retirement; it's about enjoying life and the freedom it brings. Many people aren't financially prepared for retirement, but with good planning and knowledge, you can be confident in your readiness. I encourage you to start planning for retirement today to lay the foundation for a fulfilling and secure future. It is God's will for you to be prosperous.

> Deuteronomy, 8 :18
> "you shall remember the Lord, your God, for it is he who gives you Power to get wealth that he may confirm his covenant that he swore to your father, as it is this day"